FUTURE

C000219961

MORE FOR INSPIRATION ONLY

A.R. ACADEMY EDITIONS

MORE

FOR INSPIRATION ONLY

FOREWORD

IN 1996. HERE YOU CAN SEE MANY
WORLD OF NATURE, TECHNOLOGY
GRAPHICS, PEOPLE, COLOURS,
ENDLESS. IT IS SOMETIMES FRIC
OR NATURE CAN ACHIEVE. AR
COURSE ONLY A MARGINAL FRAC
PROOF THAT CREATIVITY IS ABSC
BACK TO BEAUTY. I PITY PEC
RICHNESS. MILLIONS OF PEOPL
THEM. THIS BOOK IS NOT FOR T
DIRECT LINK BETWEEN INSPIRAT
FOR FUTURE SYSTEMS OFFICE TH
PART OF THE EVERYDAY CREA
STUDENT OF ARCHITECTURE, DI
THIS BOOK I WILL BE A HAPPY MAN

'MORE FOR INSPIRATION ONLY'
IS A CONTINUATION OF 'FOR
INSPIRATION ONLY' PUBLISHED
1ORE IMAGES FROM AROUND THE
H E MILITARY, PLANES, CARS,
SHION, PLANETS. SOURCES ARE
TENING FOR ME HOW MUCH MAN
ITECTURE AND DESIGN ARE OF
ON OF ALL THIS. HERE IS ALSO
UTELY ESSENTIAL ALL THE TIME.
LE WHO CAN'T SEE ALL THIS
HAVE EYES ONLY FEW CAN USE
M. FIRST FEW PAGES SHOW SOME
N SOURCES AND OUR PROJECTS.
IS AN ESSENTIAL AND NATURAL
VE PROCESS. FINALLY IF ONE
IGN OR ENGINEERING CAN USE

JAN KAPLICKY, 1999

STRUCTURE

AUSTRALIA II

ALUMINIUM YACHT

1983

PROJECT 221 LORD'S MEDIA CENTRE 1994

STRUCTURE

KINETIC

AERIALS ON

M 998 JEEP

KINETIC

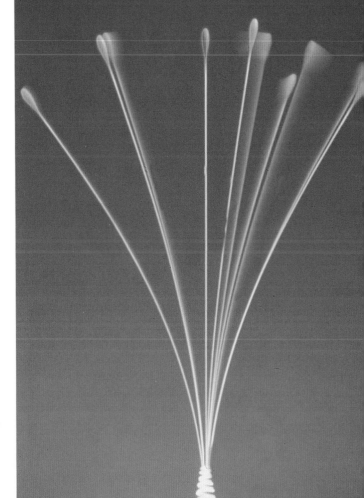

PROJECT 246
CONSTRUCTION
TOWER
PENDULUM

FLY'S EYE

LIGHT

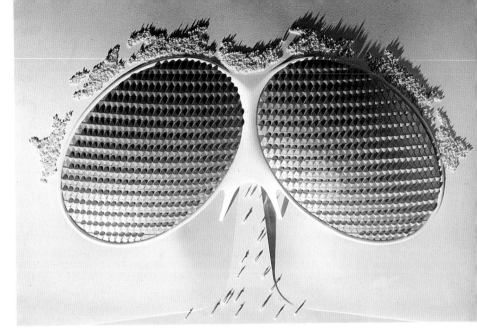

PROJECT 224 EARTH CENTRE 1995

LIGHT

BUNKS SUBMARINE U.S.S. PORTSMOUTH

SPACE

PROJECT 175 BOATEL 1990

SPACE

SHARK TAHITI

FORM

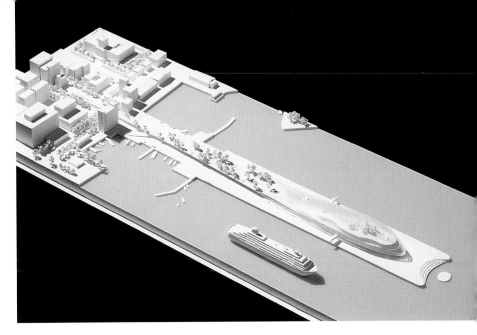

PROJECT 217 YOKOHAMA PORT TERMINAL 1994

FORM

MAGINOT LINE BLOCK HOUSE 1933

INVISIBILITY

PROJECT 222 SEASIDE HOUSE WALES

INVISIBILITY

CARLO MOLINO TABLE 1949

ELEGANCE

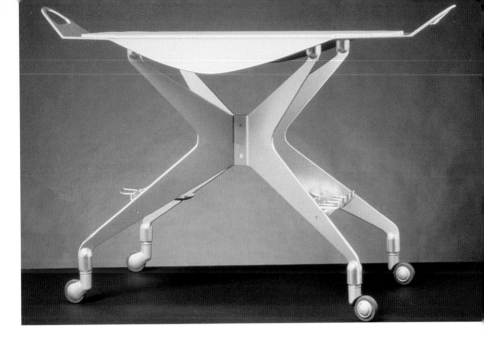

PROJECT 178 IVY TROLLEY 1990

ELEGANCE

JAN KOULA CUTOUT AVENUE 1897

IDEA

PROJECT 209 MEMORIAL PRAGUE 1993

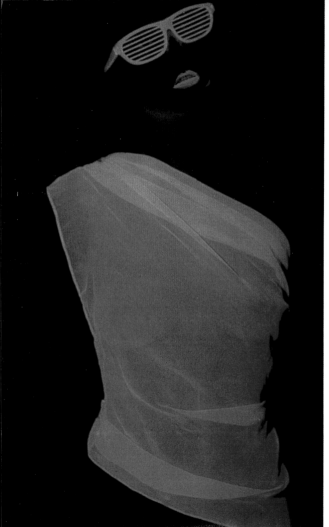

GREEN LADY

COLOUR

PROJECT 219

DOCKLANDS BRIDGE

1994

WILLIAMS RUTAN V - JET II PLANE 1997

CONSTRUCTION

PROJECT 216 JOSEF K HOUSE 1994

CONSTRUCTION

TOHATSU 6 ONE DESIGN INFLATABLE BOAT

COMFORT

PROJECT 237 DINGHY SEATING 1996

COMFORT

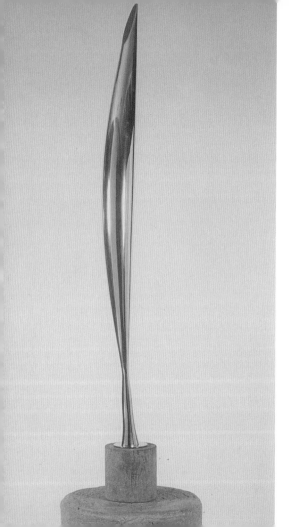

IMAGE

C. BRANCUSI 'BIRD
IN SPACE' 1927

IMAGE

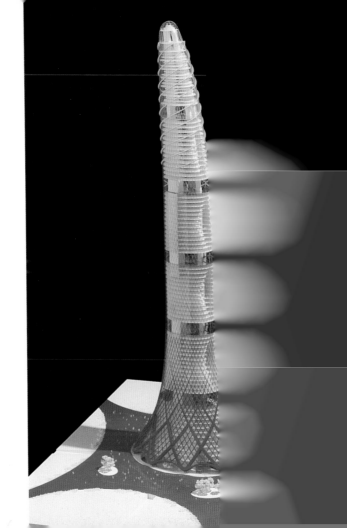

PROJECT 176

GREEN BIRD 1996

IMAGES

BRAVE MAN

JOHN GLENN

ASTRONAUT 1998

'1 071489   94 4 8 08:22 11SEP98 £0.60 Adult

sport   Not transferable   London Transport   Not transferable   London Transport   Not transferable
        Retain ticket for inspection   Buses   Retain ticket for inspection   Buses   Retain ticket for inspection

7839   Valid to Lancaster Gate Stn. (7,10)

LONDON TRANSPORT BUS TICKET 1989

ELECTRONICALLY PRINTED

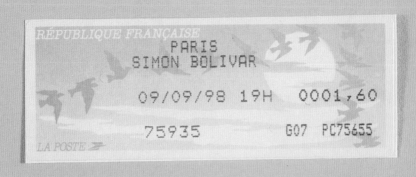

RÉPUBLIQUE FRANÇAISE
PARIS
SIMON BOLIVAR

09/09/98 19H   0001,60

75935   G07 PC75655

LA POSTE

NEW STAMP FRANCE 1997

OLD FUNCTION NEW IMAGE

LIFE

BETTE DAVIS

JANUARY 23, 1939 **10** CENTS

LIFE MAGAZINE

COVER 1939

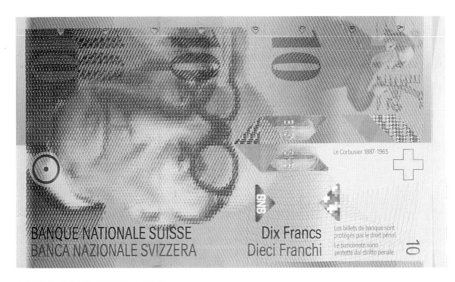

BANQUE NATIONALE SUISSE
BANCA NAZIONALE SVIZZERA

Dix Francs
Dieci Franchi

Le Corbusier 1887-1965

Les billets de banque sont protégés par le droit pénal.
Le banconote sono protette dal diritto penale.

10

SWISS BANK NOTE 1997

MODERN BANK NOTE

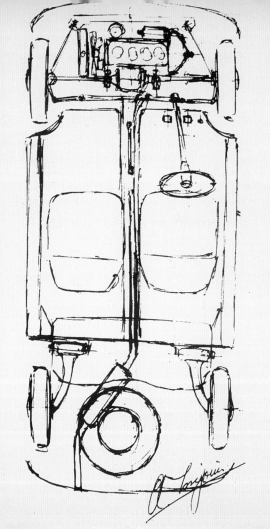

**UNIQUE
DESIGN OF
THE UNIQUE
CAR**

ALEC ISSIGONIS

AUSTIN MINI

SKETCH 1957

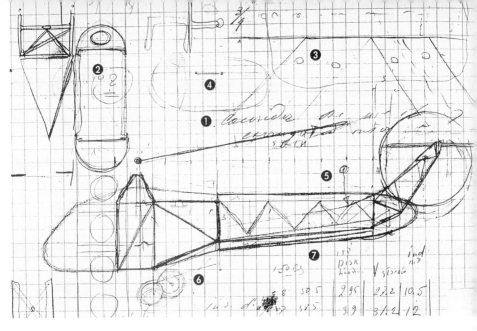

SIRORSKI XR-4-A HELICOPTER 1941

CONCEPTUAL
SKETCH

PEBBLES

BEAUTY UNDERSTOOD BY FEW

WATER

COLOUR, COOLNESS, TRANSLUCENCY AND
MUCH MORE

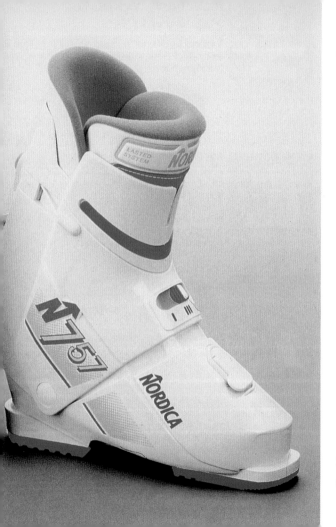

NORDICA N 757

SKI-BOOT 1990

**NEW FORM
FOR NEW
THINKING**

IMAC POWER PC 63

COMPUTER 1998

U.S. ARMY

MESS TIN 1917

MANY YEARS
OF EVOLUTION
OF FORM AND
FUNCTION

DIETR RAMS

BRAUN

SM3 SHAVER 1960

ELEGANT
DECORATION

FORD GRANADA CAR
WHEEL 1991

44

THOMAS TC 100 TABLEWARE 1961

STACKABLE, FUNCTIONAL, SOPHISTICATED DESIGN

COMPLETE
PROTECTION

DECENT
EXPOSURE

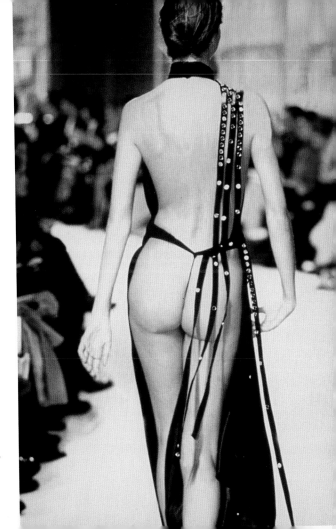

OCIMAR VERSOLATO

DRESS 1997

REVOLUTION
DESIGNED BY
ENGINEER

FIRST BIKINI 1946

FEMALE BODY

SECOND AERODYNAMIC SKIN

SPEED SKATING SUIT 1994

COLOURFUL
REVOLUTION

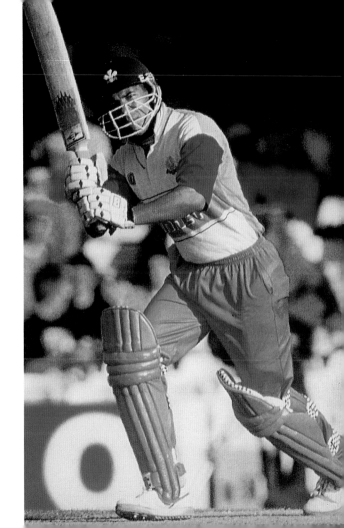

ENGLAND'S

CRICKET PLAYER

1996

BEST FOR
VERTICAL
DREAMS

E.S.A. SLEEPING

BAG 1995

CONFIDENCE
IN DESIGN
AND
MATERIALS

CLIMBERS' TENT

FOR 2 1997

FILM 'LA VOCE LONTANA' 1933

VISUALLY STRONG

FILM 'TOP OF THE TOWN' 1937

INTERIOR WITH AN ELEGANCE

LIFE NINE
DAYS OLD

HUMAN FETUS
9 DAYS

COORDINATION OF MOVEMENT POSTURE AND BALANCE

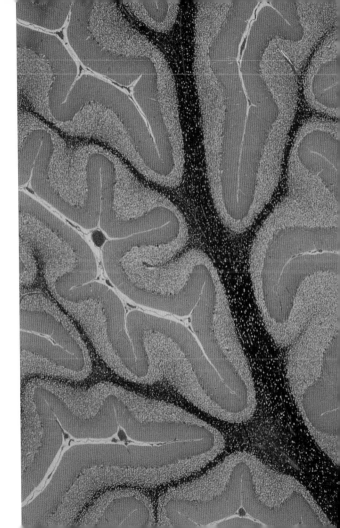

THE CEREBELLUM

OF THE HUMAN

BRAIN

ABB SOCIMI GROUP EUROTRAM STRASBOURG 1994

OLD IDEA NEW FUNCTION

MAGNETIC LEVITATION TRAIN JAPAN 500 KM/H

SPEED OF PROPELLER DRIVEN AEROPLANE

C. JENATZY 'LA JAMAIS CONTENTE' ELECTRIC CAR 105 KM/H 1899

GREEN CAR 100 YEARS OLD

PEUGEOT 'TULIP' ELECTRIC CAR 75 KM/H 1996

PAINFULLY LONG EVOLUTION

OTTO LILIENTHAL BIRD WING GLIDER 1896

FIRST FLYER

VOITURE A VAPUER 1771

DANISH ARMOURED CAR 1945

IMAGINATIVE IMPROVISATION

AEROSLADE TATRA V 855 1942

OLD BODY FOR NEW FUNCTION

N.A.S.A. HUBBLE

SPACE TELESCOPE

1990

INTERNATIONAL SPACE STATION 2002

LIVING AND WORKING IN OUTER SPACE

'PATHFINDER' SOLAR POWERED UNMANNED AIR VEHICLE 1995

NEW POWER FOR NEW TASK

HONDA 250 GP MOTORBIKE

MAN BIKE GRAPHICS AS ONE

ARAB NOMADIC TENT

**ORIGINAL INSPIRATION FOR ALL TENSILE
STRUCTURES**

'JURTA' MONGOLIAN TENT

CERTAINLY NOT EIGHT CORNERS INSIDE

BATEAU MOUCHE PARIS 1981

MORE BUILDING THAN BOAT

SUPERSTRUCTURE OF 'KALA KALA' STREAMLINED FERRY 1935

NEW FUNCTION FOR ADVANCED STRUCTURE

UTILITY
SPACE BY
FAMOUS
ARCHITECT

MALLET-STEVENS
'NORMANDIE' 3RD
CLASS CABIN 1935

7 4

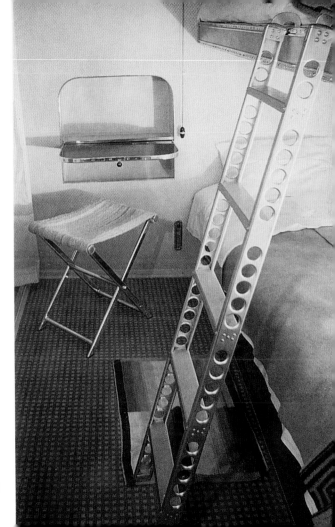

WEIGHT AND
FUNCTION AS
MAIN DESIGN
CRITERIA

GLAF ZEPPELIN II

AIRSHIP CABIN 1936

BOLLARD SYDNEY HARBOUR 19TH CENTURY

SCULPTURE WITHOUT SCULPTOR

FORM

FOLLOWS

FUNCTION

CZECH

BLOCKHOUSE BELL

AJ 5N 52.5 TONNES

1938

REFUGE HUTS SOMALIA 1992

OLD TRADITION-MODERN MATERIALS

HOMELESS PEOPLE UNITS COLON PANAMA 1990

NOT DESIGNED BY DESIGNERS

GENERATIONS
AND
GENERATIONS
OF
REFINEMENTS

ARAB BOAT 1991

PALM TREE LEAF BAHAMAS

CENTRAL SPAR AND RIBS

NATURAL BRIDGE ARCHES NATIONAL PARK UTAH

NATURAL BEAUTY

A2 AMPHIBIOUS BRIDGE BUILDER GERMANY 1968

CROSSING IN A FEW MINUTES

U.S. ARMY DROPPING PLATFORM WITH SHOCK ABSORBING PALLETS   1992

IMPACT FORCE

VOUGHT A-7 E CORSAIR IN PRESERVATIVE COVER

PRESERVED FOR ETERNITY

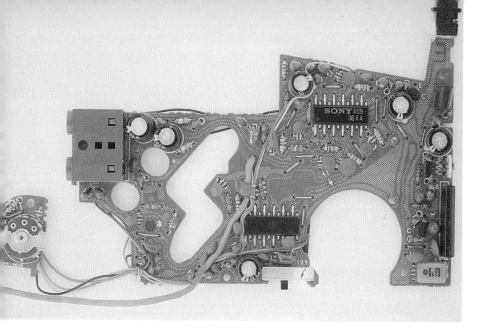

SONY WALKMAN PRINTED CIRCUIT 1982

MINIATURISATION

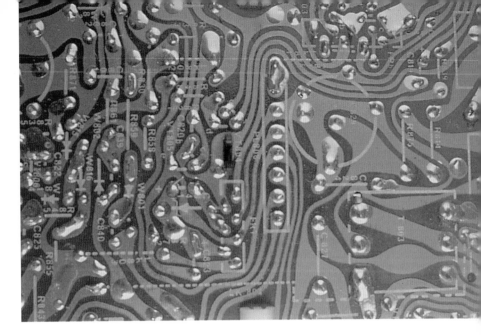

CIRCUIT BOARD 1995

INVISIBLE POWER

MCDONNELL DOUGLAS 300 PERSONS MACH 2.4 TRANSPORT 1996

AFFORDABLE SUPERSONIC TRAVEL

LOCKHEED MARTIN TIER III STEALTHY PILOTLESS AIRCRAFT

MAN MADE OBSOLETE

SUPERMARINE SOUTH HAMPTON MK 1 FLYING BOAT FUSELAGE 1925

VERY SOPHISTICATED WOODEN STRUCTURE

TOO HEAVY
FOR UNIQUE
PERFORMANCE

'ENDEAVOUR' J
CLASS STEEL
STRUCTURE YACHT
1934

91

CRASH TEST OF 'SMART' CAR

NO TESTING IN ARCHITECTURE

SAVING LIVES

AUDI CABRIOLET

AIR-BAG

J.S. SCHLAICH SOLAR COLLECTOR AND GENERATOR SAUDI ARABIA 1985

POWER FROM OUTER SPACE

RADIO TELESCOPE ARECIBO PEURTO RICO 306 M

LISTENING TO OUTER SPACE

68.5 POUNDS
OF
SOPHISTICATED
MATERIALS
AND
ENGINEERING

PEDAL POWER
'DAEPALUS' 1988

WEIGHT,
DURABILITY
AND
REPAIRMENT

GROB 6520 T
COMPOSITE
FUSELAGE 1992

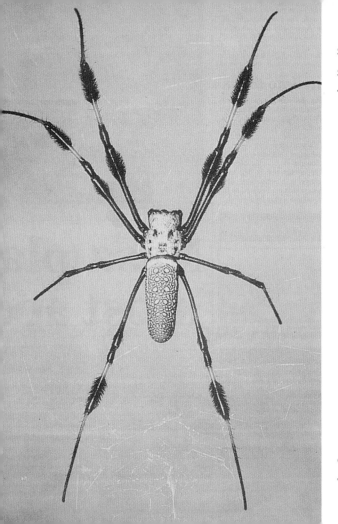

**SPIDER SILK
STRONGER
THAN STEEL**

GOLDEN ORB
WEAVER SPIDER

MANTA RAY

UNIQUE FORM

STAR FISH

COLOURFUL INSPIRATION

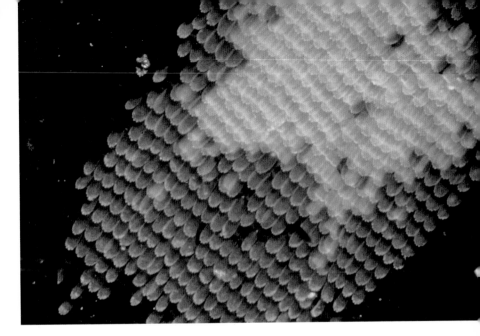

TROPICAL BUTTERFLY WING

SOPHISTICATED COVERING

LAUNCHING OF B[...]
VIEW OF BOW.
NAVY YARD, PHILA[...]

ELEGANCE OF
FORM

BATTLESHIP U.S.S.

MISSOURI 1942

DOUBLE HULL E3 TANKER 280,000 TONNES 1995

SAFETY FIRST

LOCKHEED F-117 NIGHT HAWK STEALTH FIGHTER 1977

INVISIBILITY EVEN ON THE GROUND

CZECH BLOCKHOUSE N-S82 'BREZINKA' 1935

COLOURFUL DESTRUCTION OF THE SHAPE

'LA CALOBRA' ROAD MALLORCA SPAIN

PROTOTYPE FOR A BUILDING

R. MAILLARD SALGINATOBEL BRIDGE 1930

COMPLIMENT TO THE COUNTRYSIDE

V.G. SUCHOV 60M

CABLE MAST

NIGRES 1927

SUPER TANKER 'ECO AFRICA' IN VENICE

OLD AND NEW IN COMPETITION

RUSSIAN 'VICTOR' CLASS SUBMARINE AND COUNTRYSIDE

NEW FORM OF BUILDING

LZ. 127 GRAF ZEPPELIN IN BRAZIL 1936

POWER OF THE FORM

WATER, FORM,
TREE AND
HORIZON IN
COMPLETE
UNITY

THOMAS CHURCH
GARDEN SANOMA
CALIFORNIA 1948

112

RYOAN-JI TEMPLE KYOTO 1488

MUCH MORE THAN BEAUTIFUL

BUNGLE BUNGLE MOUNTAIN AUSTRALIA

CITY OF THE FUTURE

NEW
URBANISMUS

CORAL CROWN
TUAMOTU
ARCHIPELAGO
POLYNESIA

LAVENDER FIELD PROVENCE

COULD BE A BUILDING

PADDY FIELDS AILAO MOUNTAINS CHINA

INTERACTION OF STRUCTURE AND TERRAIN

PEOPLE'S PROMENADE

CHARLES BRIDGE

PRAGUE 1357

HERTFORD PLACE PARK LONDON

MINIMAL SIZE WITH MAXIMUM PLEASURE

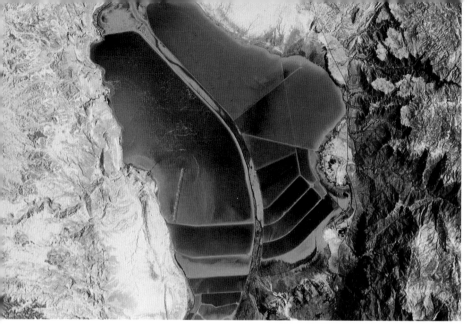

DEAD SEA EVAPORATION FLATS FROM SPACE SHUTTLE

NEW URBANISTIC POSSIBILITY

SATELLITE SHOT OF RUSSIAN AIRCRAFT CARRIER FROM 300 MILES

SHOT WHICH CHANGED A HISTORY

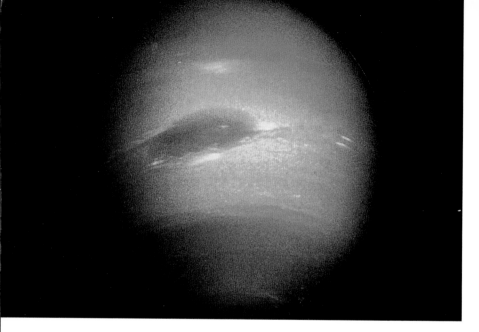

PLANET NEPTUNE BY VOYAGER 2 1989

NEVER SEEN BEFORE

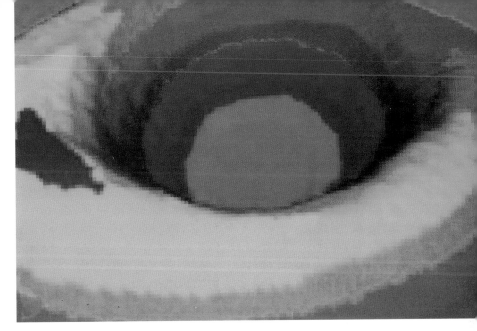

COMPUTER GENERATED ANTARCTIC OZONE HOLE 1996

BEGINNING OF THE END

DASSAULT F1 'MIRAGE' FIGHTER AND RONCHAMP CHAPEL

ARCHITECTURE AS LEADING FORM

UH60 'DESERT HAWK' HELICOPTER AND CAMELS SAUDI ARABIA

GENERATIONS APART TRANSPORT

C. BRANCUSI 'SCULPTURE FOR THE BLIND' 1916

ULTIMATE MINIMAL FORM

STUNNING
FORM WITH
MISSING
DECORATION

WOMAN'S HEAD
CYCLADIC
2700-2500 B.C.

FIRST PUBLISHED IN GREAT BRITAIN IN 1999 BY
ACADEMY EDITIONS

A DIVISION OF
JOHN WILEY & SONS,
BAFFINS LANE, CHICHESTER,
WEST SUSSEX, PO19 1UD

ISBN 0 471 98770 0

PRINTED AND BOUND IN ITALY